NEVER TO BE THE SAME

The solitary soldier made his way to the aircraft which would take him to a land where soldiers are transformed and then return where they pretended to be: the person their parents knew, their girl friend loved, and the person they use to be. The soldier prayed to our Lord: "Lord, I don't want to pretend to be the person my parents knew, and my girlfriend loved. I want to be me.

DEDICATED TO THE MEN AND WOMEN WHO

SERVED THEIR COUNTRY IN VIETNAM

CONTENTS

5

DOOBER

THE BASEBALL GLOVE

LIFE HAS BEEN GOOD

DAY AFTER DAY

LOVE ONES' WITH NAMES ON THE

WALL

GOOD-NIGHT JIM BO

FAMILIES WITH THE NAMES

OF LOVE ONES ON THE WALL

REACHING OUT

ACKNOWLEDGEMENT

I wish to thank cousin Betty for her encouragement and continued belief in me. My wife for her patience and understanding.

A very special thanks to my friends who would stop and listen to a sentence or paragraph with comments of that's good, keep it up, you've got something there, and my favorite, did you really write

Thank you, Russ, for your help!

AUTHOR   ROGER VANOVER

A SOLDIER IN VIETNAM 1970

''

THE YOUNG RECRUIT

Before church service began, the pastor announced a young man was leaving today for basic training in the marines. he announced to the congregation. Just as soon as he made the announcement, it left my mind, but then decided to stay. I started thinking about the time I left for basic training. It was fifty years ago.

The Vietnam War was consuming the psyche of the nation, and there were different opinions about our nation's role in the conflict. When I graduated from college, my future was already planned.

My pastor once said to me: "Brother, when the Lord wants you to move, you move." I realized the Lord wanted me to go and speak to this young man. A youth leader mentioned it again to the congregation before the service ended.

I stopped on my way to lunch, and no one was there, but on my way home I saw them in a parking lot saying their goodbyes and stopped. While walking toward the family, I didn't recognize anyone but the youth leader. We greeted each other, and I asked: "which one is Will? He pointed to the young man and I began walking toward him when I realized my voice was gone. Lord, let me talk and say something encouraging. I said something but don't recall one word. It must have been okay.

I can remember my time in Vietnam and wanted the young man to know he was loved by his family and friends, and that he had the respect of a grateful nation.

INTRODUCTION

I woke up in the early morning and remembered my dream. During the night, someone had taken a picture puzzle of my life, shown it to me, and then threw it down. "You can put it back any way you wish." I wanted it back the way it happened. My life had been good, even with the valleys, where I didn't qualify to bottom fish and my mail was addressed: RESIDENT: 100 Lodebar Lane.

My mother made sure my brother and I went to Sunday school, wore clean clothes, and changed into our play clothes after school. My father was a coal miner who worked double shifts because he knew a lay off loomed on the horizon. Our family grew up in a time of feast and famine; it was the way of coalmining families.

I can't recall needy families or wealthy ones, we were all the same. It was like believing in Santa Claus until you found out

14

the truth, and even then, you didn't want anyone else to know you knew.

My Santa Claus believing ended when my favorite teacher gave our senior class a survey which asked how many bedrooms in your house and how big it was. The next balloon burst after high school graduation, when I rode in a small foreign car called a Metropolitan with my uncle to a place everyone at home called the promised land.

When I arrived I saw asphalt paving, shopping centers, and lots of cars. There wasn't any mansions and streets of gold like the Lord promised in the Bible. I knew immediately this place was given the wrong name by the folks at home. My first job in the promised land was emptying garbage cans into a garbage truck. Any ambition I possessed needed to come out in this place. Like the Jefferson's, I was determined to move on up. What does this have to do with Vietnam Journal, Reflections, and Personal Memories: everything.

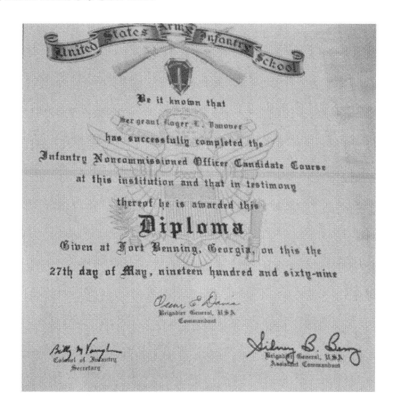

COME TO BED AND GET SOME REST

I can't sleep because of that war.

"It was fifty years ago," she said.

"I know how long ago it was, if you remember,

I was there, and there are some things I need to settle."

"You need to let it go," she said, with love in her heart.

"I will: I promise, just give me a little more time, your love and understanding.

I'll sign a peace treaty with those who fought against us in the war.

We all fought for a reason and justified it every day. The next war our country has, let the politicians fight until they don't exist anymore."

Good Old Boys Having Fun

Secret training on Red Onion, a make- believe military base, and we took vows of silence at the Poverty House. Lyndon Johnson and Barry Goldwater, 1964 presidential candidates, was the starting point and we argued to the point of exhaustion. "Now what should we call you beautiful ladies?" We'll call you Senorita and Vanilla, we don't want to give away any family secrets.

We headed to the Cranes Nest River with thoughts of glee for a night of ecstasy. We listened to music from Nashville on the car radio and we drove Pontiac GTOs' we thought would always last. The summer nights on the riverbank received a five-star rating.

We had a secret code when the town policeman was on patrol and it was time to go; one of us would say, "Here comes Harlow, we were cool." This was what we did the summer we went to war.

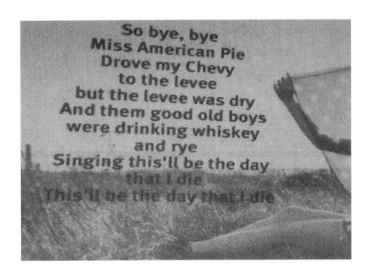

So bye, bye
Miss American Pie
Drove my Chevy
to the levee
but the levee was dry
And them good old boys
were drinking whiskey
and rye
Singing this'll be the day
that I die
This'll be the day that I die

When I returned home from Vietnam, the nights on the Cranes Nest were a faded memory and Señorita and Vanilla were no longer in town. They had found some other good old boys to show them around and the GTOs' we prized didn't mean as much. I needed time to recover from the war. We would laugh and have fun again. It just took longer for me.

"When Johnnie comes marching home

We'll give him a hearty welcome then"

"The ladies they will all turn out…

When Johnnie comes marching home

When Johnnie comes marching home

When Johnnie comes marching home."

MR JOHNSON'S WAR

The air was thick the morning the aircraft circled and finally touched the ground. We were soldiers, sent to fight a war, and a reminder wasn't needed when it stopped on foreign soil.

They called us grunts, a badge of honor, and we were now in Vietnam, to fight someone else's battle.

There were those who walked off the plane but made the trip home in a body bag. Cruel you think, but in war, it happens. We were led into a room and given the tools of war; bayonets, hand grenades, and a book on jungle survival.

A colonel walked into the room and gave a patriotic orientation I didn't need to hear. I've heard ones like it many times before. "The hell you say," I heard myself mutter. "I'm here, and I'll fight your war, but I'll do my own thinking, thank you, sir."

"Young man, you should be ashamed," I heard someone saying. "But you don't understand, I muttered. This is Vietnam, a different kind of war."

The names of the K.I.A.'s was carved on the Vietnam Wall, and others made a pilgrimage to see those names, shed tears, and wonder why.

Good-Bye

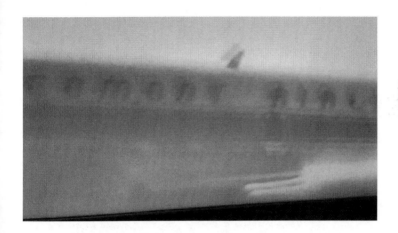

    The Piedmont jet waited for passengers to load and I gave my mother and father a hug and a final goodbye. Walking to the plane, I waved once more as my brother captured the moment. Processing for Vietnam started in Oakland, California, where new arrivals received booster shots, fatigues, and jungle boots. During my time in Oakland, I discovered a friend from high school and we were processed for our journey together. Three days later we boarded the plane for our destination. Having a friend next to me was reassuring. The only stop, Anchorage, Alaska, and the flight from there went to Bien Hoa Air Base.

There was a muted conversation on the plane and silence when the pilot announced entrance into Vietnamese airspace. One shared thought among many of the troops was home. Would we see it again? I don't know what went through my mind. The jet landed the door of the aircraft opened as troops slowly walked to the door and walked even more slowly off the plane. When my turn came, I looked to the left and saw body bags on a nearby aircraft and then smelled the stench of the air and watched smoke from the huts slowly filling the early-morning sky.

This scene is etched in stone in my memory. We were given an orientation and then rode to Long Binh for assignment. My orders were to join the 199th Light Infantry Brigade, Second Battalion, Third Infantry, Company D. I had no knowledge of the unit and asked someone about them. "They work around Saigon."

It didn't sound too bad. There was someone else there: Viet Cong (VC) and the Thirty Third North Vietnamese Regiment (NVA).

Riding with me in a truck that day to join our unit was a young man from California. We didn't talk; it wasn't necessary. The next time we made a trip together was November 10, 1969. We joined our squads and our platoon made its way into the jungle. My first memory of contact came as we lifted off from a clearing and the chopper received fire. We settled down for the night and I slept on the ground with rocks as my mattress. It wasn't the best accommodations, but it was "home sweet home" for a long time.

I often use the word "rubbers" in my journal as a reference to the rubber trees and plantations in our area of operation, III Corp, Long Kahn province. It consisted of Long Binh, Saigon, and Xuan Loc. October 1969 was my first full month in the country as a squad leader. There were night ambushes in the rubber plantations, attachment to mechanized tracks with the Eleventh Armored Cavalry, and reconnaissance patrols for signs of VC. It wasn't unusual to find sleeping positions or deserted base camps left by the VC and NVA.

On October 12, my squad was down to five men because of sickness and leave, and our platoon was dropped into the wrong landing zone (LZ). I wrote: "Humped for three hours and it is hot. I am carrying a heavy load…We finally link up with our company and set up our night defensive position (N.P.D.) with the platoon. At 2200 hours that night, there is a B52 raid 800 meters from our location. I don't think they know we are here. Raid finally over." It was a crazy day.

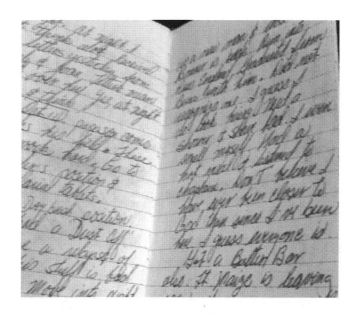

The next day we went to an LZ to return to Fire Base Vernon and waited for the choppers for an hour and a half in waist high water before they arrived. It was a good feeling to leave the jungle. My squad picked up two new guys when we returned to Vernon where I saw a classmate from college.

My appearance didn't resemble the picture in my college year-book. I had several weeks of beard and jungle fatigues so dirty they could stand up by themselves if taken off." When the

29

time came to set up for the night, the rain came and made everyone miserable. Letters from home lifted my spirits as I read and later replied. It was a way to reconnect with family and friends. Night-time was the worst for me; I lay and thought of life that was different from what I experienced here.

During October my squad rotated from location to location in the rubbers. We received our share of sniper fire from the VC there and discovered a 105-artillery round that had failed to explode and detonated it.

Staff Sergeant Standard joined the platoon during our final days in the rubbers before moving out to the jungle. Everyone called him Frag Daddy because grenades were all over his fatigues. His knowledge of jungle warfare came from a previous tour, and I learned a great deal from him.

The platoon left the rubbers to the jungle and set up for night ambush by the river; it was a beautiful area; my admiration of the scenery stopped when the VC shot at us and the sounds of AK-47 rounds went over our heads. It ruined my day.

I walked point several times. The position was the most exposed and dangerous place in the formation. It was lonely, the jungle was thick, and your next step could be your last. If you walked into an ambush, the point man was in a vulnerable position. Orders from headquarters were: "noncommissioned officers are no longer to walk point."

HOW DID IT HAPPEN

There was an uncanny rhythm and sameness to time in Vietnam, but individuality existed. Every grunt had a story, memories, and the desire that went beyond the insanity of war.

I talked with each member of my squad to know each other. The unifying bond was survival; it didn't recognize race, religion, color, or political view. I graduated from college, taught, and found myself in Vietnam as a combat squad leader. I'm still in disbelief when reflecting on this.

My journal contains prayers to a God I hadn't accepted, a background I didn't appreciate, a girl who became my wife. God's vision for me went beyond the insanity of war and my ability to comprehend.

32

There was no way a boy from Little Doc Phipps Holler, the name of my section of town, could survived the madness of war without God's guidance. When I accepted this, there was no longer any questions or mystery.

I AIN'T GOING

Humping through the bush for days in Nam got monotonous. It was a time to reflect, and a million thoughts ran through my mind, but I stayed vigilant for the sudden burst of gunfire that would come. I was thankful when it didn't.

When a new day began, I wondered if this was my last and whether I would go home in a flagged draped coffin as a symbolism of my unspoken patriotism. When my time came to walk point, I needed a clear head to spot trip wire, booby traps, and mines.

The days were hot and humid, and when the time came to set night position, it rained, and everything was soaked. The next morning began in silence as I walked a trail and found signs of Charlie. (The military name was Victor Charlie but called Charlie by the grunts.) The silence ended when gunfire erupted, and the sounds thundered through the jungle, as RPG's exploded, and I heard the "crack, crack, crack" of AK-47's as bullets flew over our head. I returned gunfire emptying clip after clip in my M-16, and then it stopped. I waited for the call, "Medevac. Medevac." I shook, and in the brief silence, smoked a cigarette,

We had been in the bush for what seemed an eternity when the platoon leader informed the company we were going to a forward firebase for stand down and a much-needed shower, clean clothes, write letters, relax, and go to the NCO club. The Vietnamese band played songs the grunts remembered from the world. The night ended as the band played "I Left My Heart in San Francisco" and the grunts joined them, remembering a place called home.

Reality returned the next morning when the platoon arrived at the helipad to prepare for combat in the jungle. We filled our packs with rations and canteens with water and C-4. a plastic explosive the soldiers used for heating our meals and loaded all the ammo and grenades we could carry.

Our destination was an LZ in the jungle to begin the hunt for Charlie or his hunt for us. Huey (our nickname for the UH-1 series of helicopters) were ready to lift off and the platoon leader signal to board.

Above the noise of the helicopter blades, I heard the platoon leader yell, "Let's go Jones." He yelled again, "Get on the chopper Jones." The solitary figure responded: "I ain't going." The Huey lifted off for our destination without Jones. I looked down and saw him watching his comrades disappear into the horizon. I never saw him again.

Jones was a good soldier and followed the instructions of his squad leader. Why did he choose to take this path, only Jones knows; he defended his country when called and he, and he alone, will defend his actions. I state these observations as his squad leader.

NOVEMBER 10th. 1969

There wasn't any combat area of operation where you could relax, but the time in the jungle was one of the most intense. The events from the end of October to November 11th, 1969, were memorable for many reasons.

The platoon began an operation that ended in tragedy for a family and a moment I live with every day. It started with a river crossing where we used the rope from our hammocks, and air mattresses to cross a river; choppers dropped the remainder of our equipment on the other side.

The platoon began a journey that went deeper and deeper into the thick jungle. We discovered sleeping positions and bunkers as well as deserted base camps. By the time we left the area, our platoon had gone through the jungle foliage and swamps. The platoon finished its mission and was airlifted to a rear area where we received clean clothes and showers before going back into the jungle.

The brief respite ended where it started, our return to the jungle. When the platoon landed in the LZ, my squad went on a cloverleaf recon while the rest of the platoon moved in another direction and immediately made contact. It was brief, and there were no causalities. The platoon found rice, uniforms, and RPG's left behind by the NVA. A feeling of uneasiness was with me the entire time.

At the end of our second day, we set our night position. When I began my guard duty, I heard movement to the front and reported the activity several times. There wasn't a positive or negative response to my report. In my mind it was, "Keep listening," "Get back if you hear anything else," "Are you sure?" The movement finally stopped. I have asked myself should I have done more, been more demanding, or expected more from the command post. Maybe memory even betrayed me, because I felt guilty about what happened next.

When the morning came, we were ordered to move out of the base camp to another location. As I reached for my pack there was a loud explosion and I fell to the ground as blood ran from my face. The sounds of gunfire filled the air, and my platoon responded. I knew I was hurt, but alive and gave thanks to God for allowing me to live. A medevac arrived and hovered over the canopy of the trees and a basket dropped from the chopper. I heard someone say, "You'll be okay Teach." I was lifted off the ground for the safety of the medivac. The medics lifted me out of the basket and made me comfortable as another wounded soldier was placed into the chopper. The medevac then began its way to a field hospital.

41

THE FIELD HOSPITAL

Medical personnel placed me on a gurney, and my mind went numb to events which occurred earlier. A nursed approached me, and I remember only one question. "Do you have a next of kin we can inform?" My reply was "yes."

I later learned a telegraph was sent to my parents informing them I was wounded. The local western union office was in a funeral home. There is a sense of irony in this to me. I waited for someone to inform me of my condition. From this time forward, I can't recall what happened. I awaken and found myself in a hospital room, my face numbed and covered with gauze from surgery. Later, a colonel presented me with a purple heart. Even today the events are difficult to comprehend.

While In the hospital, a first cousin came to see me, and you can imagine my surprise when he walked in the room. A member of my squad was recovering from malaria and asked to borrow twenty dollars. I was surprised when it was repaid. It's strange what I remembered.

THE LETTER

The medevac's flight to the field hospital was silent except for the chatter between the pilot and the triage unit at the hospital. The rhythm of the chopper blades was hypnotic and had a calming effect as my thoughts wondered. I glanced at the still figure lying quietly at my side, no one needed to tell me his fate. I now knew his identity and thought back to the time we rode in the back of the truck. Neither one of us could have foreseen this moment. I knew little of his personal life and was surprised when the letter arrived from his wife wanting to know what happened.

I couldn't find the words or courage to answer her. I struggled many years with why I lived, and a fellow soldier died.

I don't know when or where I was when I received my answer. It wasn't my decision to make. Like Job, I questioned God. He didn't owe me an explanation, nor should I have expected one. As a Christian, I am to live by faith and accept God's will.

THEY DON'T SEE HIM THE WAY HE USE TO   BE

I see people every day and want to say to them: "I'm not the person I use to be. Once I was quick on my feet and could throw a baseball where it needed to go. No one can see me that way today.

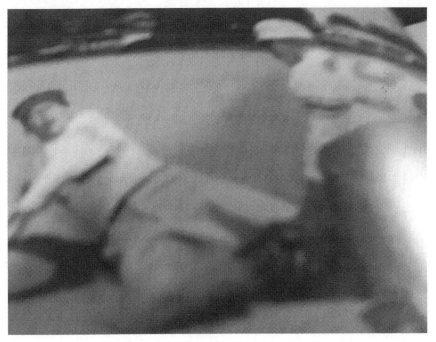

I was told: "Your one heck of a musician." My reply, "I don't practice anymore

I was a soldier in Vietnam, a place where most people can't even find on a map. They don't know the story of the dark granite wall. I shed tears when I think about it today. How sad I think, how sad. There are times I believe a part of me is buried there still.

People do see an old man whose car tag holder states:

VIETNAM VETERAN.

I'll tell you something I hope people see.; a man who believes Jesus died on the cross for me. That's really what I want them to see.

IT'S FIVE O'CLOCK SOMEWHERE

During my tour in Vietnam, only once does the time bring back a memory. The squad's ambush was at the edge of a road known as a night route for the Viet Cong.

It wasn't uncommon to set ambush several hours before dark. The squad's view of the road was unobstructed. The area: a free fire zone after five o'clock made the mission intense. My machine gunner positioned himself next to me as the squad quietly watched the road. I looked at my watch, and it was 5:02 p.m. A figure came into view pedaling his bicycle with all the energy he possessed. He knew the time and was aware what could happen.

My machine gunner looked at me and said: "Teach, let me shoot the hell out of him." In the insanity of war, I whispered no. "He's a farmer trying to get home and in the wrong place at the wrong time."

51

War hadn't stripped me of my humanity. My gunner was a good soldier and was looking to me for justification to an act he also knew was wrong.

He knew my answer and was looking for justification. I've never regretted my decision.

.

ALL HELL BROKE LOOSE

The company left early in the morning on a mission and my platoon was in the lead. One squad walked in the river while my team traveled along a steep hillside. It was rugged terrain, and the company reached a place where we were to separate for a sweep.

As they like to say in the movies, "All hell broke loose," The platoon wasn't in the best position, and there were only four members of my squad that could return fire. I happened to be the lucky one in front. My location on the hillside wasn't a place you wanted when someone began shooting at you. I saw the area around me saturated with bullets.

Someone was having a bad morning, and I took it personally. I positioned myself behind a tree and returned gunfire. When the firefight ended, a medevac came to dust off an injured squad member. The medevac extracted him safely and made its way to the field hospital.

The VC had deserted the basecamp, and it was secured for the night. The encampment wasn't a candidate for a gold star housekeeping seal. The VC had left empty cans of carnation milk. When I see them in stores today, I remember that day. I thanked God for watching over me.

MOTHER HEN

I made comments in my journal about hot meals in the field and disappointment when they failed to come; the irony of this is that I don't remember any meal, hot or cold. I complained when I was out of menthol cigarettes at a time death was constant. Whenever possible, I had coffee with a fellow NCO named Snyder, and we talked; this symbolized a moment of civility for me. I watched soldiers make a pot of noodles in a helmet and marveled at G.I. ingenuity and then went to a chaplain's service and felt closer to God.

When it was time for the men to receive their pay, they complained if it didn't arrive in a timely manner, but when it came, they realized there wasn't a place to spend it.

Parts of my journal explained circumstances in such a manner that embellishment isn't needed. "It has been a long time since I've shaved and showered, and I don't even mind anymore. I look around at the men and wonder what they are thinking. I guess they are thinking about the same things I do; home, family, wives, girlfriends, and when they get to go home. "Ronnie is here by now, and William has been here for some time.

We are all here now. I had sent my friend William a letter dated October 6th,1969, which I wrote: "I do not know how long I've been here, but I do know the date. Been on an airmobile, shot at, mosquito bit, rained on, and eaten C rations. In other words, everything is normal." In a letter to William dated October 27th, 1969, Ron wrote he is in Vietnam now and assigned to his unit, the First Calvary, and will join them soon. They are near Quan Loi and serving as a blocking force on the Cambodian border. He stated he's heard there's a lot of turnover in NCO's; they don't seem to last.

The following day Ron became a platoon leader replacing the platoon's lieutenant who was killed in a firefight. The world is getting to be a place that I know exists, but it seems my world is here now. I know there is such a place because I received letters from there. I will go back one day and let history judge the morality of this war.

.

FROM MY DIARY OCTOBER 27TH, 1969:

"Rained hard last night and I don't even care anymore."
I received a new squad for some unknown reason and became
attached to them. There was Tadlock, Smith, Harry, Green, Max,
Vargas, and Andy. There would be others, but these were my
boys. I hovered over them like a mother hen does her little ones.
We would go through rough times together. The comment in my
journal on October 30, 1969: "I think a lot of my new squad."

WHAT IF

There were times in Vietnam when I made decisions, but there were times a decision was made for me because of the situation; and other decisions took on a life of their own. As a squad leader, I usually went with the platoon, but sometimes my squad was sent out on their own. I didn't want to hear: "Teach, take your men three hundred meters to the south and the rest of the platoon will hook up with you." The only tourist attractions. I remember seeing in Vietnam were points A and B.

It was late April 1970, and you guessed it--my squad was ordered to go from point A and join the rest of the platoon where we were to set up our NDP (night defensive position.

It was hot, and the recon area was in the open. As we pushed to get to our destination, our packs became heavier and heavier and the sun hotter and hotter. It turned out as the best part of the day.

After we had gone, for what seemed forever, I saw the steep and rocky mountain that awaited us. It wasn't necessary to repeat what went through my mind. My men also saw it and remained silent. After a brief rest, I said; "saddle up."

We began our climb and it became more and more of a challenge. The squad was halfway up the mountain and I could hear the moaning and cussing. I wanted to say, "Shut up you bunch of wimps," but I was out of breath and couldn't talk. God smiled on us as we reached the top of the mountain. Our climb wasn't a training film on mountain climbing. If there were VC around, they couldn't fire on us for laughing.

The terrain at the top was jungle-like growth and we rested in a secure location before we continued to our destination. No one, including myself, was a candidate for "Mr. Congeniality." We hadn't traveled far when the point found an abandoned weapon left of the trail. I honestly don't recall what it was, but it was heavy and perfect for a booby trap. I asked several members of the squad to carry it until we reached an area for proper disposal. They all refused, and I understood why. I had two choices; leave it or carry it myself. I carried it until we reached our night position.

The next morning, I attempted to stand straight but couldn't. The platoon leader gave one look my way and sent me to a forward firebase to see medical personnel; my pack and rifle accompanied me. I don't know what happened to the weapon I carried from the jungle.

I stayed out of the field for a week to recoup and during my respite I listened as President Nixon informed the nation that American troops were going into Cambodia. The next day I watched as my company and squad loaded choppers and lifted off for Cambodia. There were two members killed during the campaign. Today, I feel regret and self-imposed guilt that doesn't vanish. Life doesn't give you a redo for these situations. If it did and I were given a choice, I would have gone.

I became the new rear supply sergeant based on seniority. The current supply sergeant was going home; his tour of duty completed. I stayed in this position until I left Vietnam. I slowly became aware that the camaraderie with my fellow grunts was disappearing. It hurt, and if I had been given the opportunity, I would have stayed in the bush with them; this remains with me today.

PICTURE BY SSGT ROGER VANOVER

RESUPPLY CHOPPER BLACK HORSE BASE CAMP

STRANGE THINGS

The platoon was in a defensive position waiting for transportation to a rear firebase for a few days of rest and had called time-out from the war. Oblivious to our surroundings, a Viet Cong walked into the middle of our position holding his arms in the air and yelled Chieu Hoi," which means surrender. This V.C. missed his opportunity to become a hero; he could have destroyed half the platoon. We did make it to base camp for rest, and the prisoner, with the help of security officers, was sent for interrogation and an unknown future This incident was like one that happened to my brother.

He was serving as a security guard at Tuy Hoa Air Base in Vietnam. A VC tried to penetrate the perimeter and but was captured in his effort. My brother guarded him as the jeep made its way to security. He was a stoic figure as he pointed his M16 and dared the VC to try to escape from his watchful eye. The prisoner eyed the location of the M16 magazine and grinned. My brother looked and discovered it wasn't in his rifle. He quickly corrected the situation.

The platoon waited for the resupply chopper in a clearing at the edge of the thick foliage of the jungle. My squad protected the perimeter as we waited in the hot sun. My eyes kept getting heavier and heavier, and I nodded more than once. Suddenly, the brush to my front began shaking, and I saw something coming toward me. I pointed my M16 and was ready to fire when a deer poked its head at me and then disappeared. It was the smallest deer I had ever seen. I could have used an extra pair of under wear, but we didn't wear it.

The resupply chopper hovered above our position and began dropping much needed supplies. It was like receiving manna from heaven. Most of the supplies rolled into a bomb crater, and the men started carrying the supplies to the command post for distribution.

The pilot gave a thumb's up and began to return to his home base. A noise began emanating from the chopper like Model T gasping for its last ounce of gas. I looked up just in time to see it falling from the sky, and I heard a loud boom as it hit the ground. The pilot and co-pilot made their way out of the chopper and found themselves in an alien environment.

Strapped to their side were .45's, and I could sense their fear. The platoon leader assured them of their safety, and they spent the night with our platoon. Bright and early the next morning, a rescue chopper came and took them back to their firebase, and a Chinook, (a CH-47 cargo helicopter) lifted the down chopper just like someone had made a call to AAA.

You Buy Me Cigarettes

We approached the MP at the gate of the compound telling him our plan, "You're free to leave but you aren't allowed to take firearms." Spud and I looked at each other and walked out of the gate. To say it was a mistake in judgment was an understatement.

We started walking toward our destination with little conversation. The further we walked, the closer the jungle closed in on the road. I began feeling uneasy but said nothing. The sound of a vehicle broke the silence; it was a jeep driven by a South Vietnamese officer. In his broken English, he asked where we were going and agreed to take us.

As the jeep headed to our destination, he looked at me and asked, "You buy me cigarettes?" We aren't allowed to do that," I replied. He asked again, and I gave the same answer.

He stopped the jeep and told us to get out. I looked, and he was pointing a .45 at us. There was no disagreement on our part. He drove away leaving us on the road. I looked at Spud and he looked back at me, and we turned around and quickly headed back to the safety of our compound. There was no discussion of the stupidity of our decision.

As we made our way back, a truck loaded with South Vietnamese troops stopped and gave us a ride to our compound. The truck pulled into our quarters. Spud and I gave a sigh of relief as we climbed out. "Wonderful day wasn't it Spud?" He looked at me and laughed. "We'll do it again Teach.

THE LANDING ZONE

The squad sat in the Huey, and there was no emotion on their faces. Looking at each one, I could only guess their thoughts. They were young and still had a lifetime ahead of them if they could survive this hell called Vietnam. We all looked the same on the outside, ammo belts around our waist or over our shoulder, hand grenades placed where we could reach them, and some packed claymore mines. The emotion on their faces was a reflective and hypnotic

Looking at each one, I could only guess their thoughts. They were young and still had a lifetime ahead of them if they could survive this hell called Vietnam. The crackle of the RTO's radio broke the silence inside as the sound of the chopper blades added a harmonic background to our journey into the unknown. Each grunt held his M-16 and a loaded magazine waiting for the command, lock and load.

I learned to despise these words. They meant we were close to meeting our Savior or making it to join our waiting company in the jungle.

The time was near when the chopper pilot received the message that the LZ prep was over and the door gunner dropped smoke grenades. It was at this moment that you stopped thinking and became a soldier.

The Huey came close as possible to the ground, and you heard: "lock and load." Just as the orchestra playing the 1812 Overture, the magazine and the bullet hit the chamber in unison. My last thought as my boots hit the ground was, "Lord, help me make it to the tree line."

THE WELL HOUSE

It was a day I thought I had lost three men in my squad, called in artillery, and I used four letter words to an officer. In no uncertain terms, he informed me "never to talk an officer in this manner again." How close to me when the words came out of his mouth? I could identify his tonsils in a lineup and if he had a sister, I wouldn't date her.

The day began in hopeful anticipation. The platoon was attached to an artillery unit as a security detail. The members of the platoon could write letters and relax for a while and no beating the bush for Charlie. My positive thoughts flew away when an aide walked to the area of my squad and asked: "Is there someone here called Teach?" I won the prize again. "LT would like you to come to his tent."

My assignment: take twelve men to point A and setup night bush. The area is used by the VC for supplies and reinforcement of units. The squad, seasoned grunts, assembled and headed to the ambush site. I was comfortable with them as well as the two shake and bake NCO's. I even remember their names and during our time in the bush we became close friends. On our way the point man spotted what I called a well house. It took a half-hour to maneuver by it. We all felt better when it was in the rear view mirrow.

The squad reached the ambush site and the two NCO's, with two others, were to prepare perimeter defense as the squad took their position.

Suddenly an explosion came from the perimeter area and my heart sank. I visualized some of my squad wounded or dead. I quickly ran to the area and everyone was okay; someone had stepped on the detonation cord. The men joined the rest of the squad in the ambush. I thought to myself; every NVA and VC within a mile radius knows where our ambushed site is located. The command post insisted the squad stay in the ambush.

The squad settled in their position and a LT order me to call in artillery. The first round went over our heads and exploded. "SSgt, I'm dropping in another." The round came closer and the LT informed me another was on its way. This round knocked leaves off and several branches. I broke out in a sweat knowing another was on its way. When told, I quickly replied," no way sir." He then barked on the radio "why?" "We're down here

74

and you're not." The two of us had a conversation which I never told Mother about the language I used.

"SSgt bring your squad back to our location." No member of the squad spoke. They knew their squad leader was going to catch a mouth-full. When the squad reached the compound, he was waiting. He approached the squad and asked who was in charge. "I am sir." He got so close to me I counted his nose hair. Just another day in paradise I mumbled to myself.

The call from headquarters was welcome news. "You're to start your processing to leave Vietnam. My first thought was, "I can't believe I'm going home"; my second was," Lord, thank you and get me on that plane." I signed every paper put in front of me and left for the holding company.

While there, I saw a high school and college friend, and we traveled home together. I walked on air at the processing company and remembered a processing officer with a sideburn fetish who sent me to the barbershop three times to get my sideburns trimmed. After my third visit, I didn't have sideburns left and didn't care. I was going home. Given dress uniforms and driven to Bien Hoe Air Base, we boarded the Freedom Bird for the journey back to the world.

The plane rumbled down the runway and lifted off. It was when the pilot announced we had cleared Vietnamese airspace that the cheers erupted, and the grunts settled down for the long flight home. We made one stop in Hawaii to walk and stretch our legs. We weren't greeted by beautiful Hawaiian women in grass skirts as they danced and put Leis around our necks. I wasn't disappointed. It was better than running into a VC with an AK47 pointed at you. It was beautiful even if your view was looking through the glass in the terminal.

We were back on the jet, and our next stop was Oakland, California. After final processing, we took a taxi to San Francisco airport. The cab was crossing a bridge, and I asked, "Is this the

Golden Gate Bridge?"   "No," it's the other one, the Bay Bridge."
I could remember the walk out of the NCO club as the grunts
sang, "I Left My Heart in San Francisco." It was a time of
comradery and eludes logical explanation.

Exhausted after thirty-six hours of non-stop travel, we
purchased our tickets for Atlanta and waited for our flight. While
sitting on a bench, with the sun filtering through the window, I
fell asleep.

The sound of taps played in my ear, and I opened my eyes
to see an individual with a harmonica. He grinned, and my initial
thought of a hit across the jaw wasn't worth the cost to me. I
wanted to get home. The war was over for me. A song played in

my head as I looked for a different place to sit. It was my turn to grin.

"I'm going to lay down my sword and shield, down by the riverside, down by the riverside, down by the riverside, I ain't going to study war no more."

It began down by the riverside a million years ago, when we listened to the car radio, having fun with Senorita and Vanilla. I thought it fitting to remember when we were young and waiting to go to war.

GOOD-BYE GOOD TIME GIRL

HOME

Photo James Vanover

My father drove me home from the airport and pulled the car into the driveway and stopped. I opened the door and looked at my surroundings. The only change was me. I walked into the house and hugged my mother. "What do you want to eat?" she asked. "Cornbread, soup beans, and fried potatoes," I answered.

After my meal, I stayed in the tub for what seemed like hours, and then went to bed, sleeping until the next evening. When I woke up, I realized the nightmare was over. It had lasted twelve long months. There was no official welcome, just hugs, and kisses from my father, mother, and brothers. It was okay with me; I needed time to think and search my soul. The war still lingers in the form of scars, inside and outside, as many looks for closure. "Thank you, Lord." It's taken fifty years, but with your guidance I have closure today.

PHOTO DAVID VANOVER

W16 L87

When I saw the Vietnam War Memorial, there wasn't any more tears. It was finally time our nation needed to thank them all. A younger generation can recall, their grandfather's stories, about the names he knew on the wall. Forty-Eight years quickly pass, when you served your country, in a land that doesn't exist anymore.

The trip today was the last. My feet swell, and it's difficult to get around. I'm not the young soldier who served his country in a land that use to be. God let me live for some reason, and that's why my name isn't found on the wall. I did see my reflection in the black granite and one day I'll be called to join the names on the wall. Lord, if it's your will, put it off until I'm ready to join those names. I want to write and tell stories, and then, I'll join all my friends in Glory.

It's your call, and all I know to do is wait, until you meet me at the Golden Gate. You'll greet me like I'm someone special. You told me I was, a long time ago. You're the one who made the sacrifice, for all who call you Lord. I don't need a ticket, you punched my name a long time ago.

85

ISAIAH 2:2-4 King James Version

"And it shall come to pass in the last days, that the mountain of the LORD's house shall be established in the top of the mountains and shall be exalted above the hills; and all nations shall flow unto it.

And many people shall go and say, come ye, and let us go up to the mountain of the LORD, to the house of the God of Jacob; and he will teach us of his ways, and we will walk in his paths: for out of Zion shall go forth the law, and the word of the LORD from Jerusalem.

And he shall judge as they shall beat their swords into plowshares, and their spears into pruninghooks: nation shall not lift sword against nation, neither shall they learn war anymore."

Welcome Home Brother

I remember all of you from a long ago, and I call you friend. We have something in common, it's that place called Viet-namm. One was on a ship in the Gulf of Tokin and rode in the open sea; he's called a Blue Water Vet.

Another came to see me as I lay in a hospital bed recovering from a combat wound. I don't know where my cousin came from, or where he went when he left. His mother, my aunt, told him I was hurt and go see him. I visit you today cousin because that old place is getting to you.

You were listening to Johnny Cash in the room across the hall. We were college boys and didn't have a care." Did you and that girl you were dating ever get to Jackson.?"

You hold your head up and be proud of your service. A round from Charlie's A.K. doesn't care about your MOS. Two friends close to my heart are brave men who also served their country in that foreign land. Let's make a deal, what we all did there, we'll take it to the grave or discuss it in quite whispers. Gentlemen, I salute you, and hope someday your country remembers.

Memorial DAY

It was a heavy rain and the wind magnified the sound of the rain as it hit the side of the house. I imagined a bowling match taking place among evil spirits as they hid in the darkness of the storm. Sitting in my nest, as my wife calls my chair, I was composing an article that would appear in Southern Living and make me a household name. Writers do that kind of thinking.

The sound of thunder and the rain took me back to monsoon season in Vietnam where the days were humid, and the rain made you miserable. You never got used to it, but accepted it, and hoped Charlie was just as wet and miserable as you. I thought of other conflicts and the veterans who served from the time of the Revolutionary War to the current conflict in Afghanistan. It was okay to get wet and feel sorry for yourself I thought, you did get to come home.

I wish our country would remember and honor fallen warriors more than we do; Memorial Day is more than a day off from work or the beginning of summer. Just ask a Gold Star mother, and never say "Happy Memorial Day" to a veteran. I made my weekly trip to Walmart and was nearing the exit when I observed an individual sitting on a bench. He wore a baseball hat that proclaimed, "Proud Vietnam Veteran." I wanted to thank him for his service and inquire about his unit and time in country. Most veterans appreciate the recognition, and I wanted him to know.

"We all have a story," I remarked. He looked at me and said: "Let me share mine." I sensed bitterness in his voice.

"I had six months left when I returned home from Vietnam and was assigned to a new location to finish my tour. I was down to two weeks when a friend and I decided to take our wives to dinner and celebrate the completion of our service. We decided to have dinner in a town near the post.

Four young men stopped at our table, and one of them said: "You S.O.B.'s, your baby killers." He then spat on my friend's dress uniform; all four laughed as they walked out of the restaurant. We didn't retaliate, knowing any reaction could result in a sentence to the brig."

He finished his story, and I looked at him. He was still angry after fifty years. "I hate that town." I shook his hand and

91

said, "God bless you for your service, and may God bless you." I walked out of the store, burning inside and upset that anyone would abuse a hero. For a moment, I hated that town. Memorials exist in our nation's capital to honor the fallen. It was their sacrifice that allows all Americans the opportunity to live and enjoy our freedoms. I don't know the correct reprimand or punishment these four individuals deserve. They will answer to a higher authority one day.

SINCERELY QUANG MINH

The words were written in my college yearbook in the spring of 1966 and laid dormant until the late summer of 2017. They were like planted seeds that sprouted from the ground before the chilly winter. I was completing a memoir of a time in my life that was also buried, and decided to share with my friends, but more importantly, with myself.

After reading his words more than once, I made a call to my alumni office. After the usual courtesy of "hello, I'm," I asked if they could help me locate him. After a period of silence, a voice said: "I'm sorry, I can't find any information. Good luck with your book."

I searched everywhere for an address but with no success. I should send this story to the address given in the eloquent well wishes. The glass is always half full for me, but this one looked half empty.

Sincerely

Quang Minh

95 Chi Lang

Hue, South Vietnam

"The thirst for knowledge has given us the opportunity to become f friends and know each other Our societies are different and so are our cultures, but our needs are the same; friendship, knowledge, and love. Knowledge and friendship have abolished any barriers between us and knowledge has bought us together. May our friendship be in existence forever."

THE ADDRESS BOOK

I was searching in my desk for something, which I do quite often, and discovered a little address book which goes back to the time of President Richard Nixon. I opened it to find names of people I have forgotten and those I didn't even know. I also found the addresses of individuals who served with me in Vietnam, members of my squad and my platoon leader.

When I go out, I see old men wearing baseball hats that proudly proclaim: "Vietnam Veteran." I thank them for their service and ask: "What unit did you serve with there?" They proudly tell me, and I let them know that was one tough outfit. I sense their pride as they walk away, feeling good about themselves, knowing someone cares and remembers. Each one has a story that needs to be told before it's lost forever. I walk away and mumbled to myself; I'm glad I don't look that old, knowing God will forgive my little white lie.

I have pictures of several of my fellow grunts in the address book and try to match names and faces with little success. They are warriors who served their country in an unpopular war. A ten percent discount at Lowes and a free meal on Veterans Day is enough recognition. Most of them have seen the" Wall" and cried, some have their uniform neatly stored, waiting for the day our country will call them what they are, "Hero's!"

While healing from combat wounds, I encountered a friend recovering from malaria. It was good to see him, and we renewed our friendship, talked of the future, and promised to get together when we returned home. When the doctors gave me the okay to rejoin my unit, he presented me with a Zippo lighter, engraved with the inscription:

"May the Lord be with you always. A fellow grunt, Jim T." I still have the lighter, worn with age and time, like myself. I look at it from time to time and think back to when we were young enough to have dreams. We still haven't gotten together, he remains a name in my address book.

I have thought about her many times over the years? Someone you dated in college and now wish we had given each other time to discover our true feelings. She passed away at the age of fifty-five, still young with dreams unfulfilled. She always had a smile when and where ever I saw her. When I would ask her for a date in college, she seldom said no. I should have asked more often. I saw her for the last time while attending graduate school after my return from Vietnam. She was getting in a car with someone I knew; I just waved at her as they drove away. I was engaged at the time and felt bound by my commitment.

In the address book, she has "Captain" before her name. She was serving her country as a surgical nurse in   California. When she passed away, she was a Colonel. I will always see and feel her smile. This name in the address book is different from the rest.

Who would know a Zippo lighter would bring back memories of friendship and a smiling face that would still be with me.

THE DAY I CRIED

Anyone who served in Vietnam can remember the unique sound of the Huey helicopter. The Huey flew grunts to the landing zone and then back to a rear firebase for stand down after the completion of their mission. The medevac chopper flew the wounded to field hospitals. You couldn't go outside in Nam without hearing the sound it made. I will meet my Lord with that sound still in my head.

I was outside on a beautiful summer day working in my yard. I heard a noise from a place I wanted to forget. I looked up at the blue sky, and I saw it, a Huey helicopter. I started crying and couldn't stop. I cried and cried and cried. Then I cried and cried and cried. I finally finished and then pride took over. I wanted to make sure no one had seen me. I was Mr. Tough guy, and no one would know my feelings from the place that haunted me. It would take years before I could let it go and put it in perspective.

I've cried a lot since that day. I've cried because of sadness, and I've cried because of happiness. Today, my heart is as tender as a filet mignon. When I cry today, my tears are those of a child of God.

SHADOW BOXES

There is one, but soon there will be three. The first one belonged to my father, a World War 11 veteran. I am fortunate enough to have his discharge, and it is impressive to me. He was assigned to the Army Air Corp, the forerunner of the Air Force. He didn't discuss the military aspects of his service. I was fortunate enough to hear his stories, and I read between the lines.

There were more funny stories than war stories. My father was discharged as a private first class. I do remember comments like, "I was busted one time for..." He was 5'2", or if you exaggerated, you added one more inch. His parents considered sending him "off to jockey school." This was the phrasing used by my grandmother.

He loved his only grandson and would arm wrestle, play Nintendo, and tell tall tales to him. One was a very "tall tale." The story was in jest but taken at face value by my son. "You didn't know I shot Hitler, did you?" "Really Papaw!" My father grinned and nodded his head.

The next school day came, and he was excited to share his grandfather's heroism during the war. It didn't take long for the teacher to call home. She had admonished him for telling stories. I don't know who hurt the most, my son or his grandfather. It didn't end the tall tales, but the stories were never repeated in school. The second shadow box belongs to my brother, whose tour of duty in Vietnam was with the 31st Tactical Squadron at Tuy Hua Airbase. He was humbled by the recognition he received for serving our nation, but his service was more than any award he received. Life wasn't kind to him in his later life, but I never heard him complain.

There are stories in the shadow boxes if they could only talk. They tell the stories of a father and his two sons who served their country. My father belonged to "The Greatest Generation; His sons' country turned their back on them.

It stills hurts, but you let it go.

WHERE ARE THEY NOW

`I kept a journal in Vietnam from October 1969 until April 1970. Forty-eight years passed before I read it, and I'm surprised by its contents. I was a combat squad leader with Company D of the 199th Light Infantry Brigade, 2nd Battalion, 3rd Infantry.

When I assumed my position, I was as green as spring grass and dumb as a mule. I hope I matured beyond this during my time there. The guys in the squad called me "Teach" when they discovered I had taught. Frag Daddy and Spud were two nicknames I remember. Frag Daddy, a lifer, put grenades anywhere he could find a place and still hump. Spud was from Idaho; his nickname came easy. Tadlock was my gunner for six months; Snow also carried the M-60, and Morton was the most unpredictable and one who stuck by your side regardless. Andy's favorite was a grenadier launcher, and Morton walked point with a shotgun. All lieutenants went by L.T. Everyone else answered by their last name. I had so many RTO, I can't remember them all. No one liked a telephone cord attached to them like a strings of pearls. I was on the other side, and I didn't care for it, but it was my job.

I think of the individuals I knew during this time and those I've forgotten and wonder where they are now. I don't remember all the names, but it doesn't matter; they are still with me in spirit.

I can't believe the experiences, and more astounding, how I lived through them. I wasn't a Christian at this time, but I prayed a lot. I've heard God doesn't listen to individuals who aren't born again; I figured He let me live for some other reason.

I would like to see them all, but I learned it's better to allow the past to be the past. I'm not the only one who went through these experiences, but the memories are mine.

PART THREE   PERSONAL MEMORIES

The Other Mr. Bojangles

Have you met Mr. Bojangles? I have, and when I think of him, I grin. He didn't dance but sang in a unique voice. His laugh was infectious, and he could charm an audience with a song. I sat behind him on many performances and at the end of each song, he reached for his bourbon and coke, took a drink and said: "what are we doing next boys?" He would sing until midnight and then go to someone's home and play till sunrise. Just like Mr. Bojangles said: "I drink a bit."

He often made the statement: "I would have taken better care of myself if I had known I would have lived this long." Before his life ended, he became a lay preacher, gave sermons, and spoke at many funerals. All the way to the end, he never lost his sense of humor. He once asked a friend to get his leg out of his car. What do you say to a security guard that wanted to know why you're looking in the back of cars? I'm trying to find my friend's leg. The security guard replied: "sure, you were. Come with me."

At his funeral, the crowd was one of the largest in the history of the community. He reaches for his Perrier in heaven today and asks his heavenly band. "What are we doing next?" The answer in one voice: "WHEN THE Saints GO MARCHING IN, New Orleans style."

Ronnie started playing the trumpet with his best Louie Armstrong imitation and Lucian joined on the trombone. They were followed by Salmon (the fish) on the sax and Earl on the piano. Kenneth laid down a solid beat on the bass.

The drummer just grinned as he played, happy to be with his friends. It's not a long journey from Little Doc Phipps Hollow to heaven if you follow the Lord and stay on the right path.

Even if you get off the path he'll take you back. Some get back on the right path even without their   GPS.

MOTHER-IN-LAW

It was a Sunday afternoon after church in the late summer of 1986. My mother- in- law had given a lot of thought and prayer about the church we attended. She wanted the family to go to the evening service the following Sunday to transfer their membership. "It would be a proper time for you to make a public confession of faith." I showed no emotion but shook my head in agreement. I accepted the Lord on the 14th of September 1986. My mother- in law wanted me to be in heaven.

As I have gotten older, the answer to her prayer plays over and over as my pastor gives the invitation to the lost souls in the congregation.

I went to see her especially on her birthday. She was unusually pensive on this visit. ``Was I the cause of your divorce?" I sat speechless looking at a widow whose husband's death left an emptiness and the desire to join him. Looking directly into her eyes, I answered no. It was one of the last times I saw her, confident I gave her the answer she needed to hear. It was also the truth. She was a true lady and made every effort to understand her son-in-law.

THE HARMONICA

I received a call from the nursing home as we ate our evening meal. The voice on the other end of the line said: "I'm sorry to inform you your brother passed away at 5:20 P.M. this afternoon."

It wasn't an unexpected call. "I'll call the funeral home," I told her. I said goodbye and went numb. I had visited him earlier in the day and knew it wasn't long. Before I left, he asked me to covered him with a blanket. "I love you brother," I said and started walking out of the room. He called my name and said; "I love you too."

"I'd like to tell you something before you leave." "Sure," I replied. "I've never agreed with everything you did, but I've always respected you." This statement was the highest praise I had ever received from my brother. Life had taken us in two directions, and we lived in two different worlds. We loved each other, but a chasm existed between us. In Little League, I was the pitcher, and he was the catcher. We were in the high school band and played the drums. I never remember conflict or jealousy between us.

Our parent's left home on a Saturday afternoon to go shopping, a rare occasion for them. "You boys behave," were their last words as they left. "Sure, we will," was said in unison. They were barely out of sight when we argued. I remembered a BB gun and a BB flying over my head. The shot embedded in the wall above my head and is still in the house.

We've discussed it many times over the years, and we continued to blame each other, but can't recall the cause of the argument.

In the last two years of his life, we lost our mother and brother, and he was diagnosed with cancer. I found out about his cancer by accident and being persistent. I drove to the moon and back in my trips to see doctors with him. I'm glad God gave me the strength to make those trips.

My brother was stubborn, and no one was going to tell him what to do. This quality made my relationship with him fragile. I was walking the plank in an ocean storm and trying not to fall. I

113

had prayed before we discussed his illness and the best way to deal with financial issues that needed resolution.

On a cold November night, a friend who lived in his hometown informed me my brother was sick and needed medical attention. I got a room for the evening after driving two hours to his apartment.

When I reached his home, I found him lying in the bed. "You need to go to the hospital," It was a plea on my part. A weak voice responded: "I'll be okay." I left and came back early in the morning and told him he was going to the hospital. There was no disagreement this time.

I followed the ambulance to the emergency room and begged the doctor to admit him. In these situations, there are people you remember. A nurse entered the room and gave him an IV. I will not forget her kindness and her talk with the emergency room physician. My brother went to the hospital.

When he was released, the doctor informed me my brother needed nursing home care. I located one near his home and close to mine. There was a lot of praying during this time. The Lord gave me direction, strength, and the right words to discuss his situation. After his nursing home admission, my conversation with him was realistic, and there were no ill words spoken. From the time of his nursing admission until his death was an emotional time for me.

He accepted his situation and was aware of his condition and the inevitable conclusion. Thanksgiving meal in the nursing home was turkey and all the trimmings. A friend came to visit, and my brother was indulging in pumpkin pie. "I didn't think you liked pumpkin pie." My brother's reply, "it's Thanksgiving, everyone eats pumpkin pie on Thanksgiving. That's my brother.

I decorated his room with a small Christmas tree and poinsettia. The director of the home let me know they weren't allowed. The patients may try to eat the poinsettia, and the lights on the tree could cause a fire. Knowing his disappointment with the tree and poinsettia, I asked him if there was anything else he might want. "You didn't know I played the harmonica?" I saw his blue eyes sparkle. "No, I didn't," I responded in surprise.

I bought him the best harmonica I could find. He smiled when I gave it to him, and he laid it on a table. "I can't play it now, I'm tired." The harmonica was never opened. At the visitation, I asked the funeral director to lay it in the casket.

He rode in a Cadillac Hurst to the grave site, and I know he had a big grin on his face. He was going home to see his Mother and Father, and his brother. He grinned at me when he discovered the harmonica and I heard him say: "thanks brother"

OBAMA THE CAT

I still laugh when I remember the three of them, mother, my brother Jimmy, and the cat named Obama. Our home was in a secluded part of town we fondly called the jungle. It was an ideal place to have animals and growing up we had our share. They were just part of our life.

Mother lived by herself after my father's death and Jimmy and my younger brother visited daily. Jimmy wasn't married, and part of his routine was to visit mother several times a day. She made sure he had one delicious meal a day since he lived by himself and couldn't cook. My younger brother ran a business that occupied much of his time, but never to the extent of not checking on mother.

It wasn't long after my father's death a stray cat appeared; Mother and Jimmy adopted the stray. When I think of the situation it was symbolic; Jimmy had no one and mother needed to take care of someone. It was the best for the two of them.

I lived out of town and visited weekly. When it came to the stray cat my younger brother and I were on the same page. "Mother, if you keep that cat you'll need to take it to the vet. Her reply; "I'll take care of it." All I envisioned was my mother's death from the bite or scratch of a wild cat. They saw an animal that needed love and care as much as they did. Mother loved her boys, but she didn't need any suggestions when it came to her cat. I should have known she would let me know it wasn't any of my business what she did with her cat. Despite my pleading, the cat remained and came every day for a morning and evening meal.

I made a visit several weeks later, and mother's cat had invited several of her friends to enjoy the free meals it received every day. No one needs to guess what happened next. Later I came for a visit, and Mother informed me the stray was a mother of three cute little kittens. "We'll get rid of the little ones when they're weaned, " Mother said. She didn't want to ruin my visit. Before I left, I told my younger brother we needed to get rid of those cats before the house became a resort for every stray in the area.

In the litter was a black and white spotted kitten without back legs. No need to guess who became the favorite. Jimmy called him Obama, and I never asked why. By this time, my mind bordered on insanity as I imagined myself a cat napper sent into the world to save it from stray cats. I informed mother, in one of my rational moments, that I called animal control to come for the cats. "They're not my cats," she said, "just that one old stray; but I would like to keep Obama," Jimmy agreed, but had his plan when the animal control came.

119

One morning Mother looked and discovered the cats, including Obama, were in cages waiting for animal control to take them. About this moment, Jimmy came for his morning visit. In a very brief time, the cats, including Obama, were freed. My younger brother called and told me what had happened; I waved the white flag,

Mother died when my father passed away; they came as a set. My youngest brother died the same year as Mother; all that remained of my family was Jimmy and Obama.

Jimmy was faithful to care for Obama until the house sold. The house was a shell I once called home. Jimmy passed away two years after my brother. At his funeral, the gentleman who purchased the house came to me and said, "Obama's dead, he died from a snakebite. I want you to know Jimmy made me promise to take care of Obama." My eyes glazed-over and I said, I haven't heard any news." My wife whispered to me, " he means the cat." It all came back. I had lost my family, and now Obama was gone. It was just too much for me.

``

DOOBER

My ex-wife and I went to a local animal shelter during the early years of our marriage to adopt a dog. He was a Shepherd mix and we named him Doober. I was often asked about his name; I gave everyone the same answer, "I don't know?"

Doober grew into a large dog and became a family treasure. When my in-laws first saw him, they look at him and asked: "Do you let him into the house?" I said "yes," and they rolled their eyes in disgust. He protected our son from the moment he came into the household. Family was greeted with a wagging tail and if you looked close enough, you could see his grin.

When we moved to a new house, he came with us. In the darkest days of my failing marriage, Doober became my best friend. I brushed his coat for solitude and walked him for a chance to search my soul. I put him next to me when fireworks filled the night sky; I remembered the sounds from a distant land. The big booms came seconds later, rolling and echoing in the darkness and I pulled him closer.

Doober was older now and could barely get up and down. I had a difficult decision to make, but his suffering made it easier. I contacted a veterinarian for a date and time for her to come. I began digging his grave while he watched me from the top of our yard. When I finished my preparation, I placed a coffin in his grave and returned to the upper part of the yard where he watched; he gave me a look of understanding.

Before the vet's arrival, I asked my ex-wife to take our son and leave. The vet came and put Doober out of his pain and left me to grieve. I walked away from his grave with tears streaming as my son and his mother pulled into the driveway. He got out of the car and asked? "what's wrong Daddy?" I could barely get the words out and began crying again. I shed many tears that day. I loved that dog and never had another. Farewell, Doober my friend!

THE BASEBALL GLOVE

I had custody of a baseball glove that was twenty- eight years old. The glove was given to my son by his uncle when he started Little League. I didn't know who was more pleased, my son or my brother. I explained to my son that a baseball glove should be soft and broken in just right. "A baseball player needs to have soft hands to go with that glove." He gave me a puzzled look. A stranger might have stared in amusement as shaving cream covered the glove and rubbed until it disappeared. A baseball was placed in the glove every night to form the pocket. He used the glove until he finished Little League. His interest in baseball waned more from discouragement than anything else.

Somehow, through the twists and turns of life, it ended in my care. It survived three moves and found a resting place in my garage. I passed it day after day and didn't give much thought to its future until now. I wanted it to find a home with my son.

The glove symbolized a happier time in my life, and I hope my son's. It brings a memory of a father and son relationship we once had. I think of my son and wonder if he has happy memories of those years. I hope he does.

"Don't worry about your son and let him know you love him and are there if he needs you. He has the same God caring for him as you do, so all your worrying is not going to alter God's plan for you and your son. Everything happens for a reason, no need to try and figure it out, just accept it. God doesn't make mistakes!" Your cousin, Betty.

LIFE HAS BEEN GOOD

Life has taken me many places, and away from Little Doc Phipps Holler, where I lived many years ago. It's still one of the many places I return to visit, but only in my dreams. I went to college and got a book education. I've even fallen in love in places I've been, but ended up saying, "watch out below."

I went to war, and that's what keeps me thinking. That's an odd statement, I concede but helps me put my life in perspective. The holler still exists, but it's not the place I knew. When I look at my life, neither am I, the person that spent his youth, in Little Doc Holler.

GOOD NIGHT JIM BO

My mother made sure my brother and I went to Sunday school, wore clean clothes, and changed into our play clothes after school. My father was a coal miner who worked double shifts because he knew a lay off loomed on the horizon. Our family grew up in a time of feast and famine;

Families with the Names of Love Ones on the WALL

I can't tell you I feel your pain, but I do the best I can. It gets harder as I get older to understand why your sons and daughter's names appear on the wall instead of mine. I decided a long time ago I didn't need to know. I'll tell you what I believe; when you'll see them heaven there isn't anymore pain .

128

REACHING OUT

I find myself thinking of the same thing. It's like the movie 'Ground Hog Day.' It keeps replaying over and over and then someone said: "Thank you."

Doris / Don
Thank you!
Sincerely
Boyd

Made in the USA
Columbia, SC
15 October 2018